1/2007

MY DENTIST

by Harlow Rockwell

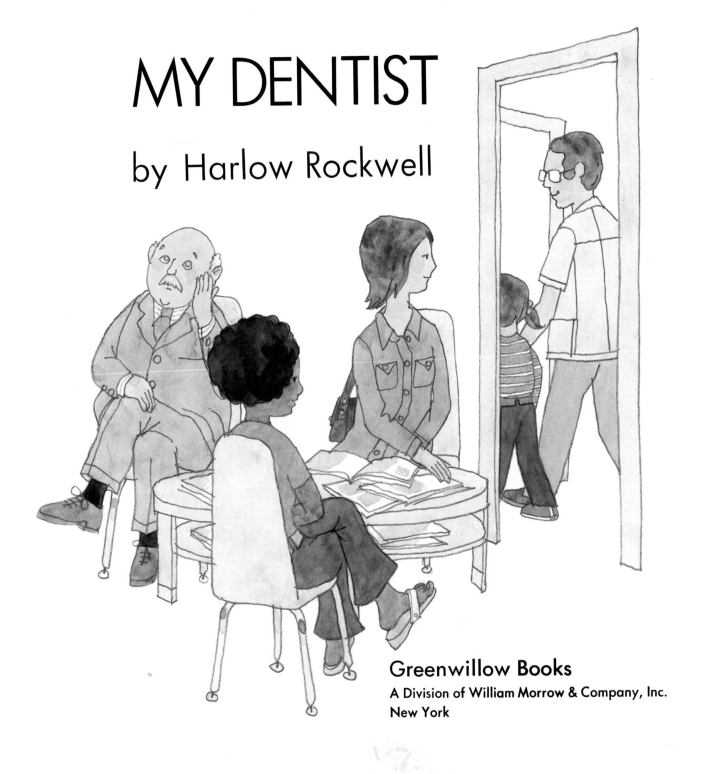

Greenwillow Books
A Division of William Morrow & Company, Inc.
New York

Inquiries should be addressed to Greenwillow Books, William Morrow & Company, Inc., 1350 Avenue of the Americas, New York, NY 10019. Printed in the United States of America.
6 7 8 9 10 11 12

Library of Congress Cataloging in Publication Data
Rockwell, Harlow. My dentist. SUMMARY: Simple text and illustrations describe a visit to the dentist.
1. Children—Preparation for dental care—Juvenile literature. 2. Dentists—Juvenile literature.
[1. Dental care. 2. Dentists] I. Title. RK63.R6 617'.6 75-6974
ISBN 0-688-80004-1 ISBN 0-688-84004-3 lib. bdg.

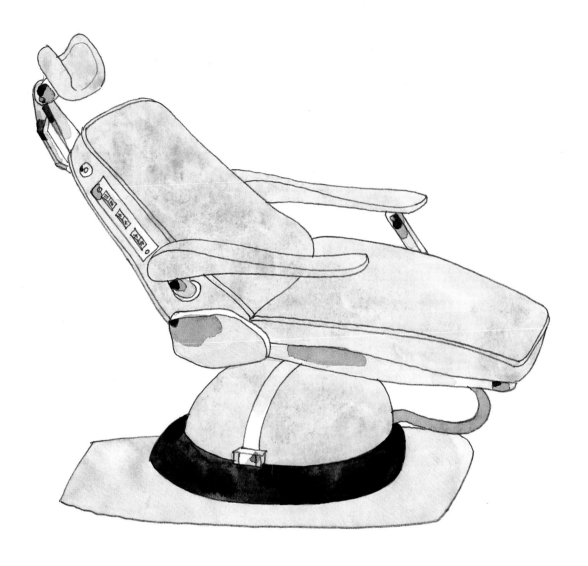

My dentist has a chair that goes
up and down and turns around.

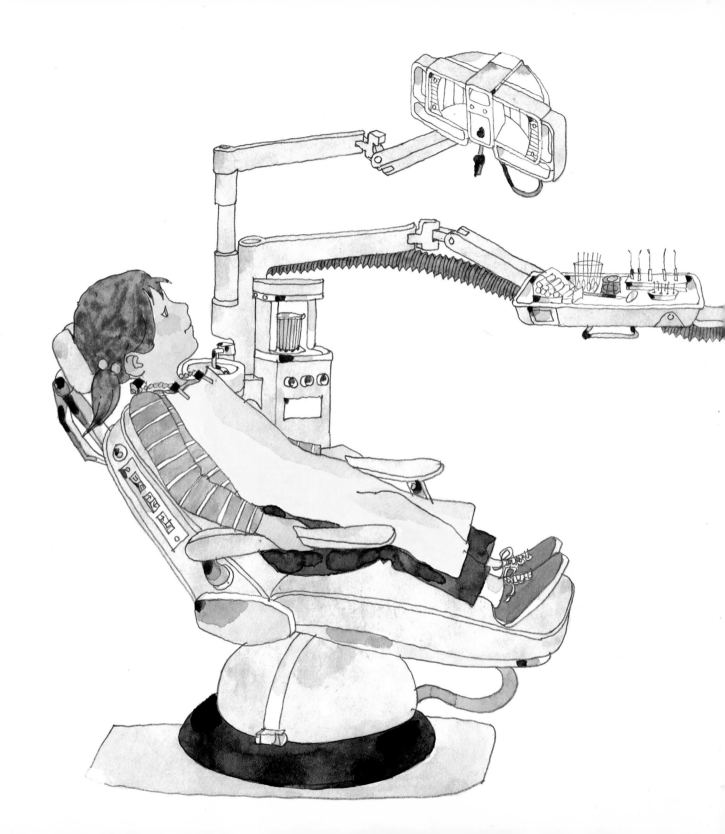

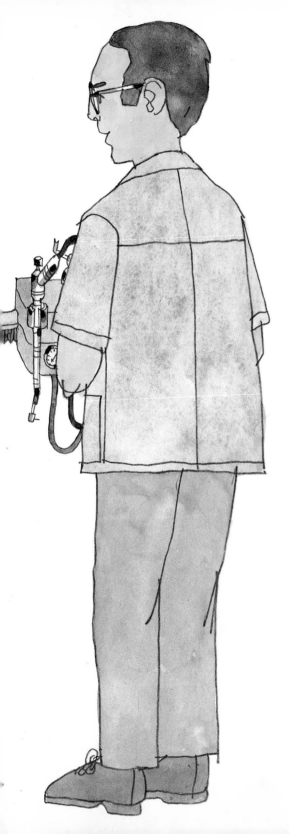

There is a place
to rest my head,
and I look
at the big white light.
I am covered with a
long plastic bib
that keeps my clothes clean.

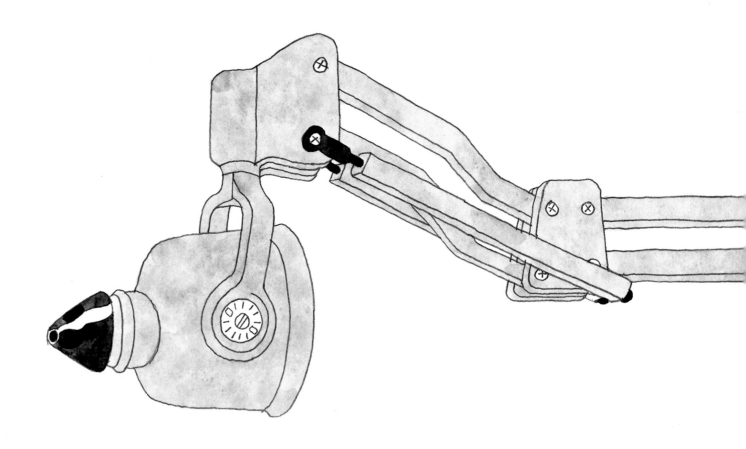

My dentist has an x-ray camera
to take pictures of my teeth.

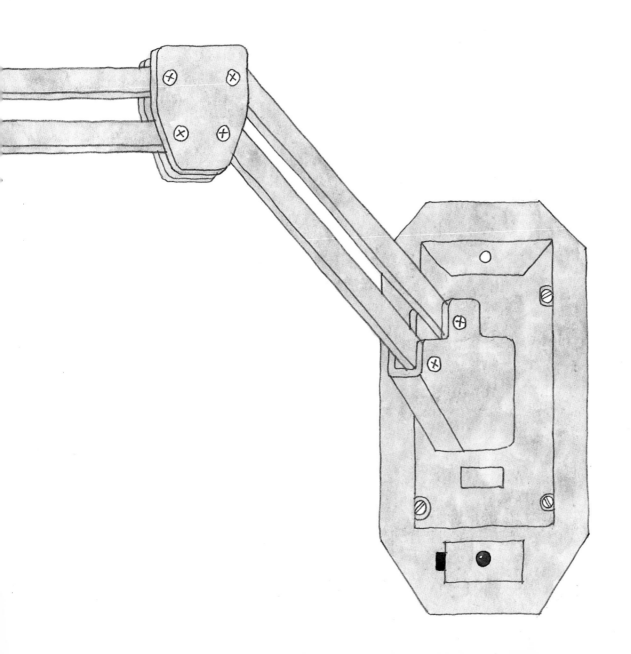

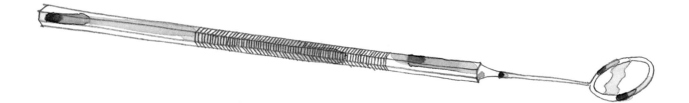

He has a little mirror
that is curved so that he can see
all the teeth in my mouth.

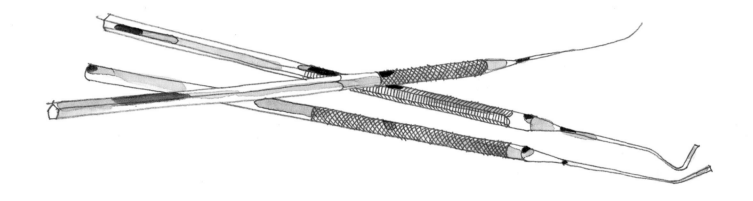

He has shiny tools
to scrape the tartar off my teeth.

He has a drill

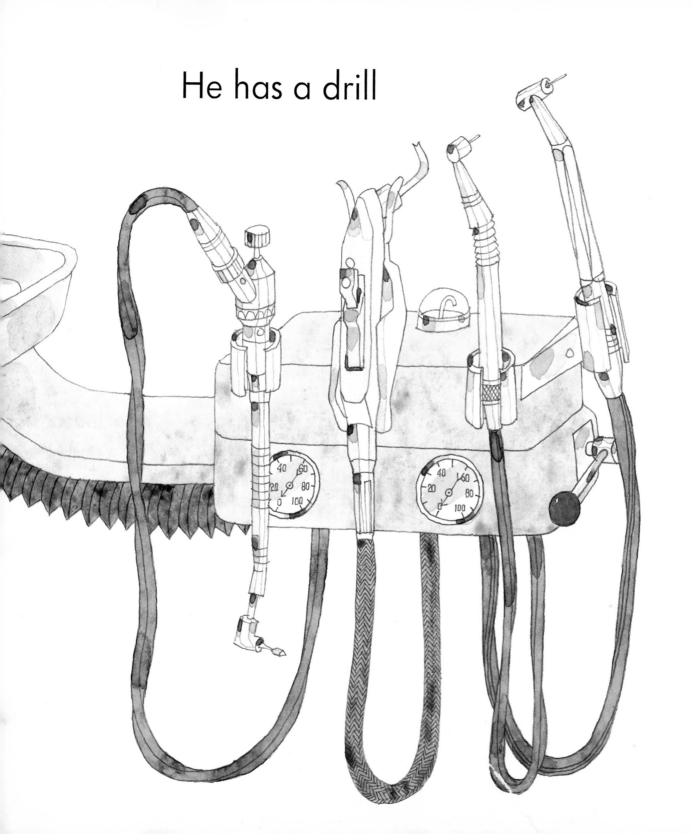

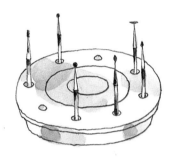

with all sorts of attachments.

Some are to fill cavities.
But my dentist says
I have no cavities today.
I'm glad.

There is a little glass pot of toothpaste.

He attaches a round brush to his drill

and brushes my teeth.
It tickles and the toothpaste
tastes good.

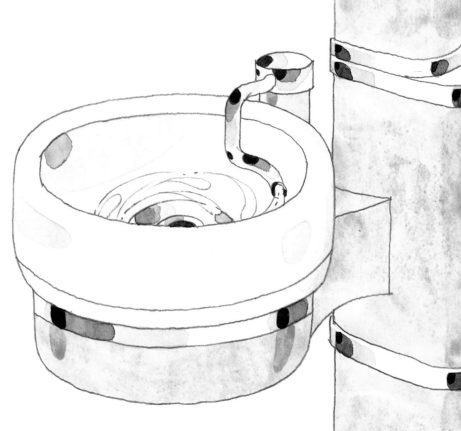

There is a small sink
right next to the chair.
Water runs around the sides
of the sink,

and there is a paper cup
filled with water.

"Rinse," my dentist says.
I rinse and spit
and rinse and spit again.

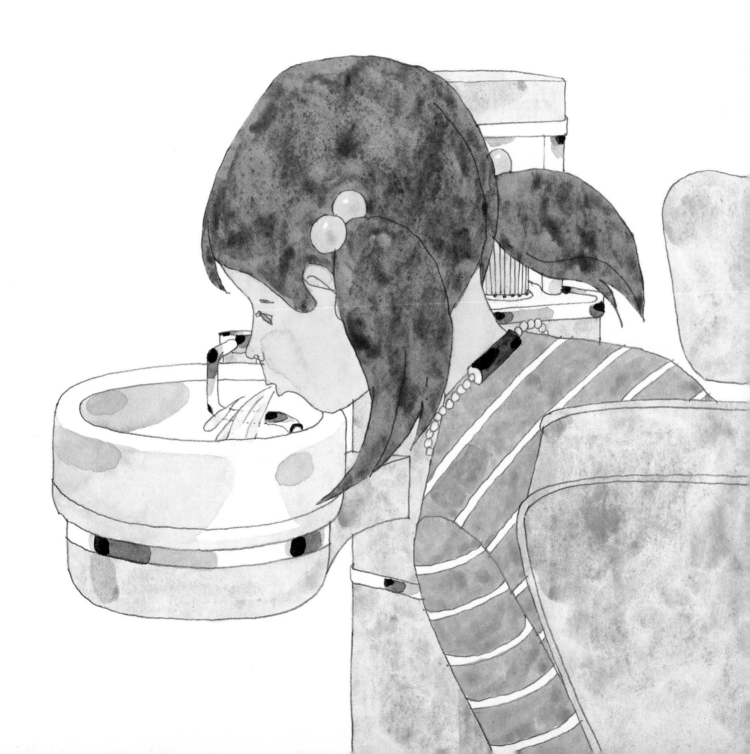

My dentist puts a rubber buffer
on his drill.

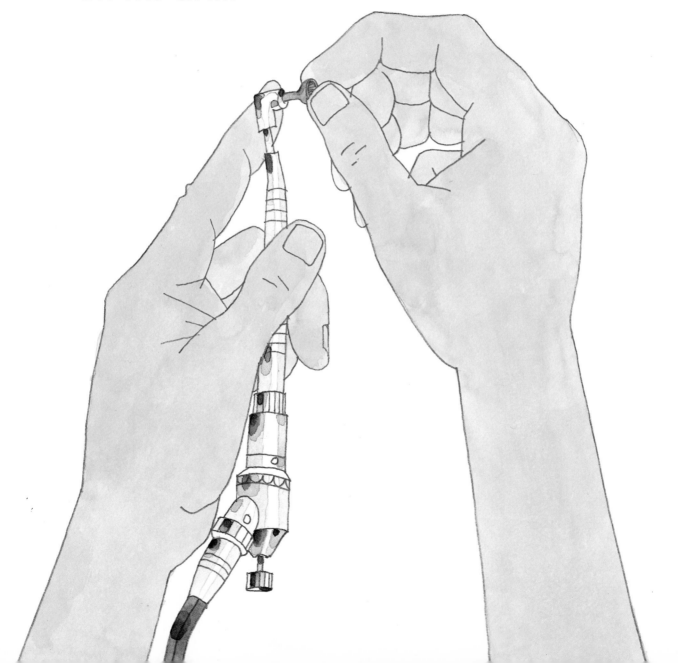

He polishes my teeth.
It feels funny, but I don't laugh.
I can't.
My mouth is open too wide.

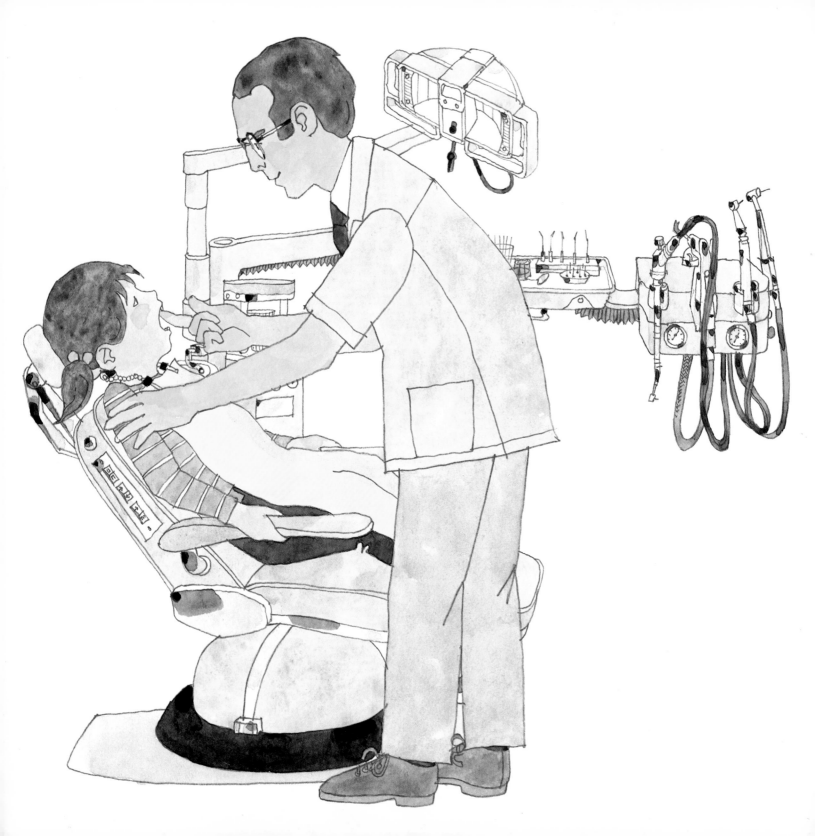

"Rinse again,"
my dentist says.
I rinse and spit again.
My dentist wiggles
my loose tooth.

He feels all my other teeth.
He looks at the empty space
where my tooth came out last week.
He feels my gum.
"You have a new tooth coming in here,"
he says.
I poke it with my tongue.

My mouth feels clean and tingly.
My teeth are smooth and white and shiny.
My dentist lowers the chair
and takes off the plastic bib.

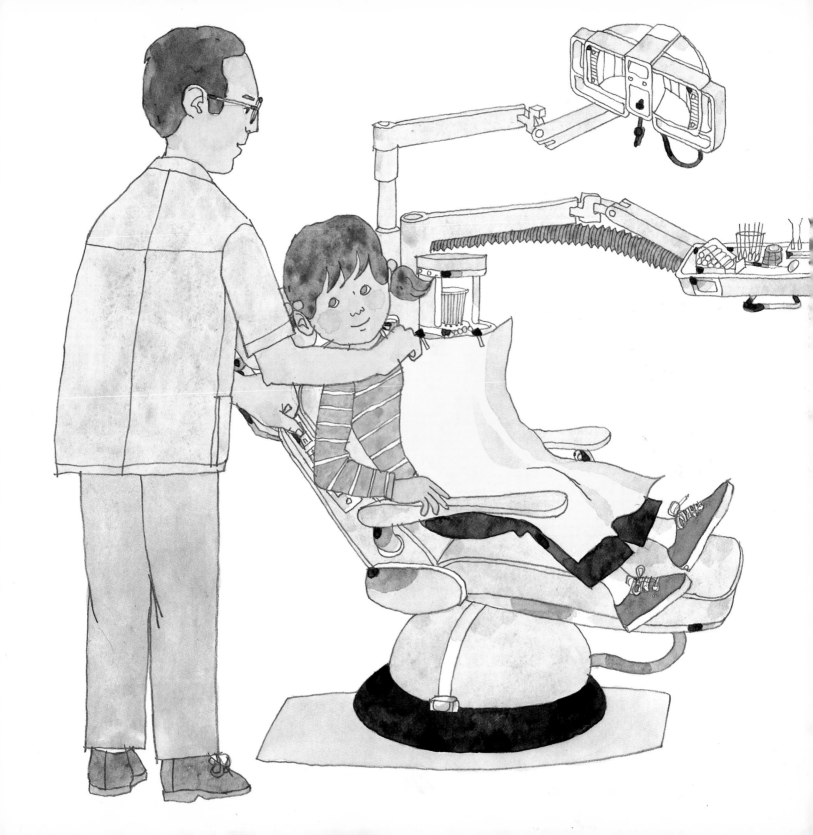

"Good-by," he says.
"Don't eat too much candy,
and remember
to brush your teeth."
Then my dentist opens
the prize drawer.
I take a water pistol this time.

And then I go home.